I'll Be DAMNED If I Say It

BISHOP AL COOK

Unless otherwise indicated, scripture quotations and italicizations are from the Holy Bible, KJV and NIV versions.

Published by Live Limitless Authors Academy & Publishing Co.

Al Cook Contact Information:

www.alcookspeaks.com

booking@alcookspeaks.com

Printed in the United States of America

Cover Design by: Adam I. Wade

Cover Photo by: Sheepish Narco Photography

ISBN: 9781732981584

Library of Congress Number: 2019936971

TABLE OF CONTENTS

DEDICATON

I must start by thanking my beautiful, charismatic, and devoted wife Debora L. Cook for her unwavering support. Your continued encouragement during life's most challenging times, your words of wisdom, and your prayers were everything that I needed to get me to this very moment. You are exemplary of *Proverbs 31:10-31;* a *Virtuous Woman.* The agape love that you've shown me has changed my life. You are my best friend and the most amazing woman that I know. I thank you for seeing the best in me, when I didn't realize it in myself. Thank you for being an amazing mother to our children and for motivating me to manifest my dream. YOU ARE SIMPLY THE BEST.

To my biological children, Alfreda, Applemania (Gregory), Altrichia (Anthony), and Tanysheia. My Grandchildren: Alnasha, Anthony Jr., Gregory III, Aliyssa, Jacquill Jr. and Kameil. Godchildren: : Tammi Gardner, Xavier Andrews, Kela Clark, Nichele Bowe,

Joclind (Joy) Smith, Rico Bell, Joe Scott, Ciara Bettard, Trenton Mclendon, Deniece Durr, Ervin Brown, Brittany Bryant, Delinah Wilson, Crystal Stephens, Shakoya Patterson, Cashe & Erica Lawson, Robert Johnson, Jr., Cassandra Speed, Elrich Bankston, Jr., Keon Broxton, Kimberly and Lamont Cheatham, Vesheka Forsett-Kurns, Tavion Stephens, Antoinette Mitchell-Dangerfield, Timani Bell, Cilia Miles, Chinesta Oda and Coach Jordan O'daffer.

Church Mothers, Imogene Crump and Marjorie Day. Honorary Pastor, Kevin "Bubba" Welch.

My Bishop, Willie L. Cook, Jr, Pastor and Godmother, Barbara Giles-Coleman, my Mother-n-law, Ida Mae Young and Apostles Charles and Frances Williams for your spiritual and financial support, encouraging words and continued prayers. To Pastor Richard Sams, you are my brother and source of inspiration! Thank you Evangelist Mary Stubbs for your prayers and support!

In Loving Memory

Father and Mother, Willie L. Cook Sr. and Elula Cook. Doris L. Cook, Eric T. Cook, Vickee L. Cook, Elder Donald Wesley, Bishop Curtis Giles, Wilma McTier, Quintero Scott, Marcus Shields, Marcus Steele, Earle Patterson, Lester Young, Paulette Brown, and Carla Booker.

REMARKS BY THE AUTHOR

I, Bishop Al Cook, would like to give honor to my Lord and Savior, Jesus Christ for the unmerited favor and mercy that He has given me throughout my life. Through His Holy Spirit, He *unctioned* me to write this book for the Body of Christ and all of humanity.

If everyone reading this book will apply these simple principles to their lives, they will get the results.

Writing this book has been one of the most rewarding things that I have ever done. Taking my thoughts, organizing them to share and inspire has awakened a sense of excitement in me that I have never felt before. My prayer for you is to employ the principles and examples in this book to your life; from your way of thinking, to your everyday conversations.

My greatest wish is for you to truly and wholeheartedly understand the power of words - *GOOD, BAD, PRETTY, UGLY, NEGATIVE, OR POSITIVE* - your words carry weight! Thank you to my Publishing and Editing Team! We did it!

INTRODUCTION

Are you familiar with Stranger Danger? *Stranger Danger* is a universal indicator that warns others of the possible threat of an unfamiliar person. Frequently taught by parents who are rearing toddlers and school-aged children, *Stranger Danger*, cautions that there is danger associated with people that they do not know.

Like *Stranger Danger*, I would like to warn you about the danger in your words and taking your words for granted.

Most can agree that before we speak, we first gather what we are planning to say by way of our thoughts. We *think* it, and then we *say* it. To truly give you an illustration of the danger in our words, I must relate it to the very experience that led me to the birth of this book.

It all started in the fall of 2004. Harmlessly, I engaged in casual conversation with a woman other than my wife on a regular basis. During this time, I didn't realize just how hazardous the dialogue was because I had allowed myself to believe that *it's no big deal*. As I reflect, I can remember how much I internally downplayed it all because never for one second, could I have imagined anything would ever manifest. This is what I like to refer to as *Stinkin'Thinkin'*. Even as a minister of the gospel, and one that had been empowered through the Holy Spirit to teach the Word of God with power and deliverance, I did not realize the weight that my words carried.

I can vividly remember that during the end of that year, I was ministering to my congregation. I heard a clear, still, voice in my ear say, *Stop Playing*. In this very moment, I recognized that the clear and *still* voice as the Holy Spirit.

When I heard it, I said to my congregation, *"Guess what the Holy Spirit just said to me? He told me to STOP PLAYING."*

In that moment, I knew very well what the Holy Spirit was warning me about.

Though I recognized the caution, even as a shepherd; a full Christian man, I failed to heed to the warning. I continued to engage in conversations with that woman. At the time, I did not realize that I had been entrapped by my own words. Those words carried weight and fortified the lust of the flesh to the point of adultery.

The very words that I initially downplayed, led me beyond adultery alone as I also conceived a child. The seeds were planted from words that initially consisted of playful dialogue. It then led to conversations that fueled a lustful spirit.

I deeply hurt my family, friends, and community. I took my words for granted and risked it all. Beyond the pain that my wife, my three daughters, and my congregation felt, I also hurt the body of Christ as a representative. People were hurt to the core.

Rearing my daughters and reminiscing on the values that me and their mother instilled in them, something that comes to mind is *"experience is not always the best teacher."* I gave the analogy to my girls, Alfreda, Applemania, and Altrichia that *"you don't have to put your hand in a rattlesnake's den to feel the pain of a snake bite."* I recall sharing with them that all you have to do is watch the agony of the person that put their hand in that den before you to learn from it.

With that said, with great understanding from my own experience, words are NOT just words. They are either life or death. Hence, from our words, actions follow. Our actions, whether they are good or bad, affect us as well as those around us.

The lesson that I learned regarding the depth of words was in a way that was hard and shameful. I am reminded through **Isaiah 61:3**, *Even in moments of ashes, the Holy Spirit can beautify it.* From this experience, not only did I learn, but it has caused me to become vigilant with the words that I speak every day. It has also enabled me and my wife to help couples restore marriages and strengthen relationships. My goal is to guide you in choosing the right words, everyday.

I thank God for His mercy and His grace. I thank Him for giving me another chance and pulling me from the depression of what my decision caused me in the year 2005. Now, I have the opportunity to empower and share insight with people all over the world to be careful with their words. According to **Proverbs 18:21**, *Death and life are in the power of the tongue: and they that love it shall eat the fruit thereof.* What the enemy wanted to use to destroy me, and take my life, God made well. Today, I have a thirteen-year-old daughter who will be fourteen this November. I am so grateful for the grace of God restoring my life, my family, and ministry. I am using my *downfall*, to help others from *falling*.

I thank God for His unmerited favor because today, I am able to use my *past* to help many others deal with their *present*.

I learned first-hand how to discipline my thoughts and my words. This book was written to help you take charge of your life by first taking charge of the things you speak and act into your life.

This book warns you to take **CAUTION AND WATCH YOUR WORDS**.

We will get results in the way we talk whether it's good or bad.

This book is very simple and straight to the point. First given to me as a sermon, the Holy Spirit then led me to transform it into a book.

He began to show me the crisis state that the body of Christ is currently in. The body of Christ speaks more about their circumstances, problems, and what we see with the natural eye rather than what God's word says about our lives.

1 Peter 3:10

For whoever would love life and see good days must keep their tongue from evil and their lips from deceitful speech.

CHAPTER 1
TALK RIGHT

The topic of this book was given to me about five years ago. At first, the *Holy Spirit* gave it to me in a sermon. After teaching the message, He said to me*, "Put this in a book."* I was inspired to title my book accordingly; *I'll Be Damned If I Say It.*

There are several sources such as Oxford Dictionary, Merriam-Webster, and even Google that defines the word *damn* as condemnation and/or to suffer eternal punishment, especially by the public expression of disapproval.

Personally, I like to define the word *damn* as hindrance, blockage, to hold back and/or stagnate.

The Lord began to minister to me about why this book is needed today for the body of Christ and all of humanity.

With our words, we truly damn our presence as well as our future.

One of the greatest things He showed me was that believers represent the largest group of people who face this particular challenge. He revealed to me that His people aren't living lives of peace, abundance, joy, love, faith or the things they truly desire. It's not because they don't deserve it, but because their conversations don't represent what they truly want. Their self-talk does not give life to what they are asking God for. I asked God for more clarity. He revealed to me that people are not living in the fullness of God's promises because they simply talk wrong. When you talk wrong, surely your actions follow suit.

He began to uncover to me that, too often, His people suffer from self-fulfilling prophecies due to the thoughts they entertain, followed by the words they speak, and the beliefs they hold in their hearts. Simply put, the lack of abundance and peace in the lives of most people come as a result of their habits of entertaining, participating in, and manifesting negative self-talk.

He guided me to **Hosea 4:6**, *My people are destroyed for the lack of knowledge.* He labored with me, showing me that His people say the very opposite of what His Word says. When we do that, we are in violation of God's Word. As mentioned earlier, we know that we are bound to have whatever we speak.

He began to help me understand how to cultivate the vision He gave me. The Lord gave me revelation in how He wanted me to describe the vision: THE POWER OF WORDS.

What are some of the conversations you're having about your life? Do your actions align with your ASK? If everything you've spoken manifested, would you be pleased?

We as believers do not always apply intent to the words that we release into the world. If you knew that whatever you allowed to come from your mouth would actually manifest, would you be more careful with your words?

When you say things like, "*you're killing me or I'm broke*" you're actually affirming those things in your life. Doesn't it make sense then to use your words wisely?

All of our lives we've been told that talk is cheap. Talk is not cheap! We have been deceived to believe that our way of talking is harmless, when in reality, it is very expensive and can cost us death.

Reckless talking and poor thinking causes believers to infringe upon the order of the Word of God. If God's Word does not declare it, then neither should we. **Matthew 12:37** encourages us, *For by thy words thou shalt be justified, and by thy words, thou shalt be condemned.*

When we speak other than what God's Word says, the enemy, who is as a roaring lion, is on the prowl. He is looking for believers who aren't speaking in alignment with what they believe. This forces you to ask yourself, *"Do I really believe?"* The enemy is hoping that he catches you slipping; operating in doubt and unbelief. It is then, that he can rob and sabotage your future. Your faith is a weapon. It's a powerful tool that stands against doubt and can slay limits. When you don't have belief, you are easily distracted by obstacles and opposition.

The enemy already knows that as believers, we have been commanded not to give place to him. We are reminded of this in **Ephesians 4:27,** *Neither give place to the devil.*

USEFUL KEYS TO HELP US TALK RIGHT

First, we must start by renewing our mind.

Ephesians 4:23 - *And be renewed in the spirit of your mind.*
Proverbs 23:7 - *For as he thinketh in his heart, so is he.*
Philippians 2:5 - *Let this mind be in you which was also in Christ Jesus.*

The reason mindset is so powerful is because it is literally the gateway to reality. Truth is, we speak what we think; what we think, we eventually become.

To keep your mind renewed daily, you have to make a conscious and deliberate decision to train and tame your thoughts as well as your tongue. Remember, if you think like Jesus you will talk like Him, believe like Him, and live like Him. As believers, we must know that what comes out of our mouths are seeds. No matter where they are dispersed, those seeds will one day grow and you will harvest them. Too often, the chaos going on in our lives is a matter of what's going on in our minds, proceed by what comes from our lips.

As human beings, we spend more time talking than we do anything else. Studies have proven that the human mouth is one of the body's most used muscular organs. That's why we have to take the Word of God very serious. We are not in a fairyland. This is real warfare. The way we talk, is not meaningless, it is meaningful.

I believe demons are constantly waiting for an opportunity to use our words against us, when they are not God-filled words. This is very real because God will not respond to anything other than His Word.

Let's review **Jeremiah 1:12**; *Then said the Lord unto me, Thou hast well seen: for I will hasten my word to perform it.*

Now, let us go back to some very important points concerning words. We as believers, can really cause our lives to be changed for the glory of God; influencing people from all walks of life. Lives can be changed! For instance, Jesus said in **Matthew 12:37,** *For by thy words* *thou shalt be justified, and by thy words, thou shalt be condemned.*

This subject is a very critical part of our lives concerning the way in which we should talk. The enemy knows that if he can get us to become weary in doing good, he can ultimately defeat us. For example, if you have been confessing a certain thing for a period of time, yet you don't have proof, don't give up or quit because we are encouraged in **Galatians 3:11***; The just shall live by faith.*

Faith is now!

You will see what you say if you stay within the principles according to the Word of God.

We have to continue to speak as if the things we are professing are already manifested.

Even we can't see it, faith is knowing that we have it. So, no matter what your situation is, or what you're believing God for, you must proclaim the VICTORY!

Another key that will help us talk right is to ensure that we are surrounded by like-minded people. Those that we converse with daily should help us live accountably. This simply means that they will 'check' you when you are not speaking fruitful, reminding us to always talk right.

Remember, **Amos 3:3** it states, *Can two walk together, unless they are agreed?* Simply put, if you are not drawing them, they are drawing you. Many people declare that they are ready, but in reality, they are not. It's so easy to say something than it is to actually live it. The main thing that separates those who *say* they are ready and those that *are actually* ready is DISCIPLINE. When you are disciplined with your words, you make a decision to die to self-every day and putting on the whole amour of Christ as we are instructed in **1 Corinthians 15:31**, *I affirm, by the boasting in you which I have in Christ Jesus our Lord, I die daily.*

Satan knows this area of a believer's life is very important and he knows that we are commanded not to give him a place. However, because we take this area of our life so lightly, it is causing us to fall short and live in defeat. You see, when you think that you are defeated, you succumb to living your life as if defeat is your truth. After operating in discouragement, powerlessness and frustration for too long, the adversary knows you feel weak and will succeed at convincing you that the best thing you can do is give up.

It's easier to convince you to throw in the towel when you've already convinced yourself that you've lost the battle.

On the opposite end of that spectrum, it is merely impossible to defeat someone who keeps getting back up. Can you imagine the willpower one must possess to get continuously get back up after being knocked down? That person has a will to win on the inside of them. Their determination to persevere is fueled by their relentless belief in their ability to win.

No matter how many times they fall, flop or fail, they keep getting up because they believe that eventually, they will experience the manifestation of victory.

I challenge you to cast down any negative thoughts that are keeping you stuck. Release those thoughts that do not align with God's Word and His will for your life. Instead, choose to believe the victorious report and God's promises.

John 8:44 tells us, *for he (the enemy) is a liar and the father of it.* His goal is to get into your head! He wants to poison your thoughts, causing you to believe that you can't win and that you should just give up. But he is a liar!

EXAMINING YOUR SELF-TALK WILL HELP YOU TALK RIGHT!

Take a moment to complete this exercise to help you begin to Talk Right.

1. Think about the last time you faced a challenge or any type of hardship.

2. During that time, what were some of the conversations you had with yourself? Be sure include the things you said and thoughts you had

3. Were your words a reflection of your DESIRED outcome?

4. One the next 2 pages, write those things down and we will revisit your Self-Talk later in the *Oh Say and You'll See* chapter!

_____

_____

_____

_____

_____

_____

_____

_____

_____

_____

_____

_____

_____

_____

_____

_____

_____

_____

_____

_____

_____

_____

_____

_____

_____

_____

_____

Colossians 4:6

Let your speech be always with grace, seasoned with salt, that ye may know how ye ought to answer every man.

CHAPTER 2
UNDERSTANDING YOUR WORDS

D o you really understand the power of your words? What we have to understand is that Satan knows that he can't do anything to a believer unless he gets permission from God. We unintentionally give him permission through our speech. I like to minister that the thing we must understand is that words are carriers. Like FedEx, UPS and USPS, whatever we release from our mouth will be picked up by one of the other carriers; God or Demons.

Jesus said in the book of **John 6:63,** *The words that I speak to you are spirit, and they are life.* This within itself ratifies that we should be speaking life-filled, productive words. We should ask the Holy Spirit to lead us to a fellowship where the Pastor has a great love for the

Word of God and a heart for the people. Ask for guidance to join a fellowship that will teach the people the whole truth of God's Word. Satan doesn't want us to take the Word of God seriously. He would love us to stay in an ignorant and unaware state of life. Being in an unlearned state of life, instead of living life as victors, we live as victims. As we know, the lack of knowledge destroys us. Therefore, in the Kingdom of God, what you *don't* know can either be very vital or destructive for us.

If you are not experiencing constant wins in your life, I'd like to encourage you to evaluate the words you're speaking. Understand, we are a people in progress which means that we may not always get it right, but we must strive to mature in the image of God. Ask the Holy Spirit to guide your tongue. **James 3:5** explicates, *We can bridle a few things but the tongue no man can tame*. It takes faith in God and being led by the Holy Spirit to help us with our talk that influences our walk. Remember, what you don't understand, you lack the ability to apply to your life. This is a very damnable position to be in, so in all your getting, get an understanding. Understanding a particular thing, helps you to know. When you know better, you are accountable to do better!

Ephesians 4:29

Do not let any unwholesome talk come out of your mouths, but only what is helpful for building others up according to their needs, that it may benefit those who listen.

CHAPTER 3
IDLE TALKING

Have you ever said something that was so foolish that immediately after realizing what you had said, you asked God to forgive you?

This is Idle Talking. When we talk idly, we are speaking foolish and unproductive words.

Let us look at the way we talk. Most people live their lives on a daily basis talking idly. Without realization, we speak words that are unproductive and fruitless. These are words that will work against you, rather than for you. For example, have you ever found yourself saying, *Lord, it seems like I will never get ahead.* This is a great example of how and why we may find ourselves experiencing financial hardship or even turbulence in our relationships. That which is coming from our mouths whether it is idle or productive, negative or positive, is taking root for growth. Too often, we get caught up in talking like the world because much of it is traditional language, however, it does not produce Godly fruit in our lives. That's why The Word encourages us in **Romans 12:2** *be not conformed to this world; but be ye transformed by the renewing of your mind that we may prove what is that good and acceptable and perfect will of God.*

To talk idle means that your words are not working for your good; they are *not* words of edification. They are opposing to The Word of God. They are words of tradition, fear, doubt, unbelief and are carnally spoken. Idle words are words of the flesh and not words of the Spirit. Earlier we ratified that talk is *not* cheap, like the world proclaims. We learned that talk is very expensive and its outcome can cost us our very existence.

The tragedy of idle talk is that we really don't pay attention to what we are saying. We take for granted the words we say, thinking that they are harmless. If we truly understood and believed how we have damned our lives as well as our children's lives and those around us, we would have no choice but to be more cautious with the everyday things we say.

Genesis 3:1 identifies the enemy as being cunning and strategic. Therefore, we must be sober and vigilant because the devil aims to steal, kill and destroy. If people you encounter are negative by nature, usually it comes from their environment or association. We must constantly evaluate our environment and be sure that we are surrounded by those that will help us to live accountable for speaking abundance, every day. Satan is waiting to hear what we have to say. He gets excited when we speak idly so that he can use our words against us because he understands how those words will one day manifest. Jesus stated in **John 6:63**, *the words that I speak, they are spirit and life.* Therefore, the greatest weapon that we possess are the words that we speak. That's why **1 Peter 5:8** instructs, *be sober, be vigilant; because your adversary the devil walks about like a roaring lion, seeking whom he may devour.* We must be on guard! Satan knows that he needs help from a believer to really bring destruction to one's life. Without co-signing with him, he has limited access to our lives.

The key to trump idle talking is to be willing to unlearn so that you can learn the process of speaking the way God wants His people to speak. We need to stay focused and sober in our minds. Consistency is another key to achieve success in the way that we speak because when we speak opposite of God's Word, failure inevitable.

Have you ever heard, "If you hang out with eight broke people, you will be the ninth one? This is because you become like those that are around you the most. It's about the company you keep.

1 Corinthians 15:33 states, *evil communications corrupt good manners.* We must pick and choose our circle of friends and associates carefully.

In many passages, The Word shows us how the tongue has so much power. For this reason alone, Satan wants us to believe that this *not* true. As we learned in **Genesis 3:1**, Satan is very clever and subtle. Apostle Paul encourages us in **Ephesians 6:11**, *Put on the whole armor of God, that ye may be able to stand against the wiles of the devil.*

Think of your tongue a light switch. As we know, each day when we flip the switch, light or darkness is the result of it. Just as light and darkness, every time you use your tongue, the words that you speak will be activating life or death. We have to be prudent of the words we speak at all times. Jesus said in **Mathew 15:11**, *Not that which goeth into the mouth defileth a man; but that which cometh out of the mouth, this defileth a man..*

We must set a watch over our mouth in order to have a blessed life. This simply means that we have to be intentional when we talk; from conversations with our loved ones, to our talks with friends. Saying things like, "*Girl you're killing me,*" from a moment of laughter, does not align with His Word.

Another worldly myth about words resonates in a popular childhood chant which says, *"sticks and stones may break my bones but words will never hurt me."* This common idiom is understandably taught to encourage children to disregard hurtful or mean things that may have been said about them. However, as adults we must recognize that not only are words painful, the power in mere words alone causes people to end their lives on a daily basis.

What we must realize is that when we error, it can be traced back to the words we have said. Stated in **Job 6:24**, *Teach me, and I will hold my tongue: and cause me to understand wherein I have erred.*

In the text, Job is asking God to teach him and he will hold his tongue because with our tongue we will speak death or life; blessing or cursing. We must, at all times, speak the language of the Kingdom of God. As we have learned, this is speaking according to God's Word. Again, Satan has three things on his to-do list; kill, steal and destroy, but he cannot operate in these areas unless we assist him simply by what we say.

David said in **Psalm 19:14,** *Let the words of my mouth, and the meditation of my heart, be acceptable in thy sight, O Lord, my strength, and my redeemer.* We have the Holy Spirit to lead and guide us. Look at it as the Holy Spirt being our spiritual GPS. Through His Word, He has given us the roadmap. Just like following the directions when we use the GPS while travelling, we must subject to His Word to lead us when we speak.

Because Satan knows that we have the ability to *calleth those things which be not as though they were,* according to **Romans 4:17**, his ultimate aim is to deceive us to believe that it doesn't work. He deceives us by causing us to believe that turbulent times are permanent and we tend to become frustrated. Easily, we begin to feel as though power is not within what we speak at all, when in actuality, we have been given the roadmap to speak life and peace during rigorous times. The key is to be patient and take necessary actions to manifest that which we've spoken.

God has given us grace. His grace has removed the struggle, giving us the blessing to declare what God has already done for the body of Christ. Therefore, when we receive His grace through salvation, we are able to walk in the authority of His Word by faithfully speaking it.

Too often, as Christians, we take this life for granted. The enemy knows that by us taking life for granted, we do not fully understand the importance of what we say. If we truly understood the importance of what we said, it would cause us to manifest continuous victories in our lives. However, the enemy would much rather us lose. The greatest tool of our warfare are in our words. Another deceptive trap that Satan throws at us to deceive us with our words is his attempt to keep us from the truth of God's Word. He will use theorist and philosophers to make us believe that speaking negatively have no real consequences, further causing us to believe that words are not a big deal. Here's the thing, you can't fool your heart. **Romans 10:10** reminds us, *For with the heart man believeth unto righteousness; and with the mouth confession is made unto salvation.* Don't get this twisted; Satan wants to keep us ignorant especially when it comes down to our words and at any given time, he will use anything or anyone to serve as a distraction.

Though the examples we have given show us the magnitude in which words can be damning, words, when spoken fruitfully can also be an investment of goodness. Just like words can hurt someone, they can also heal.

CHAPTER 4
TALK AIN'T CHEAP

Have you ever heard someone say, *"Let me speak freely?"* This is a form of traditional talk. Though we may use it regularly, truth is; words cost and they are *not* free. I think we take traditional talk lightly which is why we do not find harm in it. Even as Americans, though we've been constituted with the freedom of speech as our first amendment right, clearly, we know that things we may say, can cost us big.

So, if the truth be told, and it should be; to say words do not cost is a lie. **Matthew 12:36** informs, *We shall give an account for every idle word.* We learned in Proverbs 18:21 that words are twofold; life or death. This alone informs us that words are *not* just words.

We are in a time where we as believers are limited to what we decree because of the deception of the devil and the tradition of men have caused us to be in a place of fear and unbelief.

There are lyrics that say, "I'm coming up, on the rough side of the mountain." The word of God declares in the book of **Mark 11:23,** *For verily I say unto you, That whosoever shall say unto this mountain, Be thou removed, and be thou cast into the sea; and shall not doubt in his heart, but shall believe that those things which he saith shall come to pass; he shall have whatsoever he saith.* The hymn may fuel emotions, but it is embalmed with doubt and unbelief. Furthermore, the lyrics do not coincide with what has been written. Lastly beloved, if we are picking a side of the mountain to hike, climb the smooth side! Again, idle talking causes us to become complacent in our speech, stunting our growth.

The Apostle Paul declares in **Philippians 4:13,** *I can do all things through Christ which strengtheneth me.* So, because God said it, that settles it. On the contrary however, the enemy aims to distract and keep us in darkness as it relates to our identity. All in all, if you don't know who you are, you cannot have what belongs to you.

His goal is to cause us to think that we can only do *some* things, rather than *all* things, thru Christ.

In order to walk in faith, we must understand its use in His Kingdom. In **Hebrews 11:1** which states, *Now faith is the substance of things hoped for, the evidence of things not seen,* we are given assurance that faith is *now*. With this understood, we can identify that real faith is not predicated upon the five, physical senses. Though we cannot omit our five senses, we should not allow them to take precedence over the Word of God. Remember, faith is what you *expect* to see.

Our faith should be stronger than our senses, feelings, emotion, and what we think. It is thru these avenues that Satan plots against us, attempting to keep us out of the will of God. When we are not operating in the will of God, it is very easy to become agitated when adversity strikes. Out of His will, we find ourselves becoming frustrated and discouraged. However, to combat those feelings of frustration and discouragement during these times is to know that exercising faith requires us to believe and trust that what we are going through is temporary and *not* forever.

We are reminded in **2 Corinthians 5:7**, *For we walk by faith, not by sight.*

As we previously dissected, traditional talk tells us to *climb* the rough side of the mountain, but God's system tells us to *speak* to the mountain. Like night and day, the two *cannot* be intertwined.

We must realize that we are in warfare. Unlike WWI, WWII, and even Vietnam, this war is by far, more serious. The devil doesn't want us to know this because what we do *not* know, will cause us to live less effective as believers. His desire is for us to live like the world and be unaligned with our Godly foundation. These two systems have nothing in common with each other according to **1 Corinthians 2:14**, *But the natural man receiveth not the things of the Spirit of God; for they are foolishness unto him; neither can he know them because they are spiritually discerned.*

Through our words, the enemy's goals is to deceive us to believe that words are just words so that we further believe that talk is cheap. The enemy gets satisfaction when he hears us being lackadaisical when we speak   and talk crazy. Through the examples in this chapter, we have learned that words are powerful and expensive.

The value in our words will pay the costs of life or death. **Proverbs 21:23** states, *Whoso keepeth his mouth and his tongue keepeth his soul from troubles.* With the seriousness in the way that we talk being of ultimate importance, we must guard our mouth-gate as strong as a power forward defensively guards the basket during an NBA finals game.

When we speak, such as when the wind blows, we do not see anything. However, we do witness the results of what we have spoken as well as the effect of the wind. Though words, when spoken are invisible, the value in them are more powerful than strong hurricane winds.

God told the children of Israel in **Deuteronomy 30:19**, *I call heaven and earth to record this day against you, that I have set before you life and death, blessing and cursing: therefore choose life, that both thou and thy seed may live.* This passage alone explains how we must speak life. God told them what to choose in order to live. Therefore, this further confirms that your choices are a matter of what you verbally declare!

When a soldier is at war, they do not feel as though they are playing a game of heads or tails. Studies have proven that soldiers use strategies in order to defeat their opponent. Choosing the words to say should be taken just as serious as a soldier on active duty who is fighting for their country and their life. Talk ain't cheap! Talk is *not* a matter of heads or tails, but it is the gateway to warfare. It has been written; that you will become what you declare. When we speak in the power of the Holy Spirit, it empowers us to walk in-line with the Holy Spirit. This practice enables us walk in victory and defeat the enemy.

When we release words from our lips, we are releasing death or life, good or bad. **Mark 11:14** declares, *And Jesus answered and said unto it, no man eat fruit of thee hereafter forever and His disciples heard it.* In this passage, Jesus was hungry and came to a fig tree that looked good, but did not have any figs. Though the tree appeared healthy, it did not bare any fruit. For this, He spoke a curse on it and he went on about his business. His disciples heard him but didn't see the tree dry up right away. The next day, they passed by the fig tree, they were amazed that it had dried up and they marveled. When we release words out of our mouths they are released in the spiritual realm. Though the words released are not visible, once stated, they either work for us or against us.

As we read in the previous chapters, we must frequently evaluate our circle of go-to people. These are the people that we regularly converse and associate with. We need people in our lives that are going to keep it real with us and are willing to let us know when we step out of bound. Flattery is an enemy to us. The Word of God said in **Proverbs 29:5**; *A man that flattereth his neighbor spreadeth a net for his feet.* Flattery can be filled with deception. So, therefore, we should want people in our lives that will help us live accountably, according to God's Word and those that don't play games with us. Be careful of the company that you keep because the Word of God reminds us in **1 Corinthians 15:33-34,** *Be not deceived, evil communications corrupt good manners. Awake to righteousness and sin not for some have not the knowledge of God. I speak this to your shame.*

Let us go back a little bit and look at this way of life. In **2 Corinthians 10:3-6**, it states, *For though we walk in the flesh, we do not war after the flesh. For the weapons of our warfare are not carnal, but mighty through God to the* *pulling down of strong holds; Casting down imaginations, and every high thing that exalteth itself against the knowledge of God, and bringing into captivity every thought to the obedience of Christ; And having in a readiness to revenge all disobedience, when your obedience is fulfilled.* Warfare is in the invisible realm. We must speak the Word of God against those imaginations and spiritual wickedness in high places. Let us look at the subject in a more intimate way. Words are not simply sounds caused by air passing through our larynx. Words have real power. God spoke the world into existence by the power of his words. **Hebrews 11:3** informs, *Through faith we understand that the worlds were framed by the word of God, so that things which are seen were not made of things which do appear.*

Words do more than convey information. The power of our words can actually destroy one's spirit even stir up violence and hatred. They not only exacerbate wounds, but words also inflicts them directly. Of all the creatures on this earth, only man has the ability to communicate through the spoken word.

The power to use words is an epic and powerful gift from God. **Proverbs 12:6,** *The words of the wicked are to lie in wait for blood: but the mouth of the upright shall deliver them.* Our words have the power to destroy and the power to build up. Do you find yourself using words that empower or words that destroy? Are your words filled with hate or love, bitterness or blessings, complaining or compliments, victory or defeat?

As we have learned throughout this book, words work for us or against us. Think of hand tools. Many of the steel and wooden objects' purpose is to build and/or repair. However, they can also destroy. It simply depends on the person who is using it. Take a claw hammer for example, this is a tool that is designed to drive nails while building a structure. On the contrary, there have been instances where angry people have used this same type of hammer to destroy.

Like the examples of hand tools, words, can be used to help us reach our destiny or detour us away from it.

There is no way around it, words bring life or death. As written in **Matthew 12:36-37**, Jesus said, *But I say unto you, That every idle word that men shall speak, they shall* *give account thereof in the day of judgment.* Words are so important that we are going to give an account of what we say when we stand before the Lord Jesus Christ.

Jesus also reminded us that the words we speak are actually coming out of our hearts. **Matthew 12:34-35** states, *O generation of vipers, how can ye, being evil, speak good things? For out of the abundance of the heart the mouth speaketh. A good man out of the good treasure of the heart bringeth forth good things: and an evil man out of the evil treasure bringeth forth evil things.*

When one becomes a Christian, there is an expectancy that a change of speech follows. Being Christ-like should influence us to speak light rather than darkness. The Apostle Paul wrote in **Ephesians 4:29**, *Let no corrupt communication proceed out of your mouth, but that which is good to the use of edifying, that it may minister grace unto the hearers.* In this passage, Apostle Paul is emphasizing that one should use words that *build-up*, rather than use words that *tear-down*.

Building yourself up or finding the words to build-up a friend during challenging times, consists of words that are fruitful rather than words that are filled with negativity.

For example, instead of saying, *"I am a failure"* or *"everything has fallen apart,"* speak the words, *"I am a winner"* or *"I know things are already done."*

Paul explained that our words should build others up according to their needs, that it may benefit those who are listening. This is reminiscent of Apostle Paul's words spoken in Colossians 4:6*, Let your speech be always with grace, seasoned with salt, that ye may know how ye ought to answer every man.*

Jesus' disciple, Peter, tells us in **Peter 3:15**, *But sanctify the Lord God in your hearts: and be ready always to give an answer to every man that asketh you a reason of the hope that is in you with meekness and fear.* Peter is encouraging us to be ready to give an answer to anyone that asks you to give a reason for the hope that you have; and to do so with gentleness and respect.

Let the power of our words be faith-filled so that they will manifest and grow on good grounds. Our words should demonstrate the power of God's grace and should represent that the Holy Spirit lives within us. As followers of Christ, we should emulate the example of

Jesus. His words were filled with grace and he amazed multitudes.

Words have caused friendships of believers to lie in ruins because of words spoken decades ago. **Proverbs 17:9** states, *He that covereth a transgression seeketh love; but he that repeateth a matter separateth very friends*.

Let us take a look at **Proverbs 13:3**; *He that keepeth his mouth keepeth his life: but he that openeth wide his lips shall have destruction.* You see, the title of this book is not just a catchphrase. This title is the *Word of God* from the *Word of God* and uniquely, it does get your attention.

"I'll Be Damned If I say It." And this is so very true.

Our words are carriers that can get us in trouble or get us out of trouble. ***Proverbs 21:23***, stated *Whoso keepeth his mouth and his tongue keepeth his soul from troubles.* The world says *talk is cheap*, but the Word of God has proven its expensive value.

Proverbs 10:19

Sin is not ended by multiplying words, but the prudent hold their tongues.

CHAPTER 5
GET RID OF YOUR STINKIN' THINKIN'

Elephants are one of the world's largest land mammals. Today, there are three species that are recognized and some grow to be as big as 12,000 pounds and as tall as 11 feet.

No matter what it may be, when we think of anything in terms of B-I-G, we immediately think of strength and might!

Interesting enough, elephants that are born into showbiz, are separated from their moms to be trained.

Circus trainers spend hours a day, for months a year, preparing baby elephants for circus show day. They work to dwarf the minds of baby elephants into believing that the strength they have as babies, is the strength that they will have as adults.

Just like the conditioned mindset that trainers convince elephants to believe, we are able to do and accomplish the things that we believe that we can.

Proverbs 23:7 reminds us, *For as he thinks in his heart, so is he.*

If you train your mind that you cannot do something, you eventually believe that you can't.

Like the trainer and the elephants, the enemy tries to dwarf the minds of believers into thinking that we are not who God's Word says we are. The Word of God defines us as believers as a *chosen people* and a *royal priesthood*!

Stinkin' thinkin' causes us to lack the ability to *think* past turbulent times, hence it leaves us feeling defeated because we begin to believe that our present is our forever. How can this be when we are encouraged in **John 16:33**, *In the world ye shall have tribulation: but be of good cheer?*

The Lord knows that life will consist of challenging times, which is why he encouraged us to be of good cheer, despite what we may encounter. However, when your mindset and the way that you think is infiltrated with doubt and unbelief, being happy when adversity strikes, is few and far between.

I want to help you get rid of *stinkin' thinkin'* and I think that understanding what it means will help you to get rid of it. I like to refer to *stinkin' thinkin'* as a carnal mindset. **Romans 8:6-7** states, *"For to be carnally minded is death; but to be spiritually minded is life and peace. Because the carnal mind is enmity against God: for it is not subject to the law of God, neither indeed can be."*

Just like Michael Jordan, LeBron James, Steph Curry, Kevin Durant and Kawhi Leonard, you must *practice* casting down negative thoughts with thoughts that are of God. What we practice becomes habit and this is the only way that we can champion this aspect of your life.

The reason it is so important to get rid of *stinkin' thinkin'* is because this way of thinking is totally against Christ's way. In depth, this type of thought process is a traditional way of thinking. In **Isaiah 55:8-9** it says, *For my thoughts* *are not your thoughts, neither are your ways my ways, saith the Lord. For as the heavens are higher than the earth, so are my ways higher than your ways, and my thoughts than your thoughts.* We must keep our mindsets renewed daily so that we are able to maintain victory in our thought-life.

As we know, Satan is on a mission to distract believers and keep us from reaching our full potential. He would love for a believer to live his or her life with a carnal mindset. As we learned earlier in this chapter from *Romans 8:6-7*, this way of thinking is enmity against God.

Repeat this: I MUST GET RID OF MY STINKIN' THINKIN'!

It is a must for believers to learn how to renew our minds because it is our mind is the battleground for warfare.

In **2 Corinthians 10:5** it explicates, *Casting down imaginations, and every high thing that exalteth itself against the knowledge of God, and bringing into captivity every thought to the obedience of Christ.*

Satan knows that spiritual warfare begins and ends in our mind. Just as athletes spend time watching film of an opposing team in preparation of a game to stop and breakup plays, strategically, Satan attempts to defeat us by way of thoughts.

We must think outside the box of tradition because thoughts of tradition and thinking that "*things will never change*," is an example of how *stinkin' thinkin'* keeps us in bondage. In the book of **Romans 12: 2**, it encourages us, *And be not conformed to this world: but be ye transformed by the renewing of your mind, that ye may prove what is that good, and acceptable, and perfect, will of God.* What the Apostle Paul is teaching is that transformation comes by way of renewing your mind with the Word of God. Before you received the gift of salvation, your mindset was carnal and your thoughts were enmity to God, however, after receiving salvation, it is being Christ-like to think like Christ.

Which battlefield has had the most battles?

Our minds.

Our mind is the place where battles are won and lost. As the central station to warfare, our mind is where mere thoughts are conceived. In the enemy's pursuit to steal, kill and destroy, he gets enjoyment when we think of our minds as a *playground*, rather than a *battleground*. Of course, he knows that if we see our mind as a playground, he has an easier advantage to infiltrate how we think, thus causing us to speak reckless. This is the very reason why the Word of God has given us specific instructions on what to think on. **Philippians 4:8** encourages us, *Finally, brethren, whatsoever things are true, whatsoever things are honest, whatsoever things are just, whatsoever things are pure, whatsoever things are lovely, whatsoever things are of good report; if there be any virtue, and if there be any praise, think on these things.*

Your mind is like a receiving center, all of our ideas, goals, dreams, and plans travels through our mind. This is totally ok, however, as believers, we must be careful. Why? Well, just like going outside, and we see birds flying. We cannot stop the birds from flying over our heads, but we have the power to stop them from building a nest on our head. In **2 Corinthians 10:3-5,** we are given us the '*know-how*' on resisting the devil from developing strong-holds in our mind.

Strongholds are thoughts within our minds that holds us back. We can think of a strong holds as something that has potential to hold us, strong. Ultimately, they *(strongholds)* are thoughts in our minds that hold us back from succeeding in the Will of God. They are patterns of negative thoughts that Satan brings to our minds to distract us. This is why it is so important to cast down every thought that opposes the Word of God. If we give into those negative thoughts, we are bound to become a product of them. This is confirmed by **Proverbs 23:7**, *For as he thinketh in his heart, so is he.* We must keep our minds renewed on a daily basis and realize that this is a serious matter.

Again, your mind is where every battle starts and ends. Where every battle is won or lost and is where spiritual warfare takes place.

Beloved, a man or woman; boy or girl, can not go any further than what he or she thinks. This is what I refer to as the Law of Thinking. Throughout this chapter, we have learned how to get rid of our *stinkin' thinkin'*.

In life, a person cannot go higher than what they think. If you think that you can, you can. If you think you can't, you can't.

Proverbs 23:7

For as he thinks in his heart, so is he.

CHAPTER 6
HUNG BY YOUR TONGUE

This chapter gets REAL! You will see how you are hanging yourself everyday just by the things that you are saying!

1 Peter 3:10 reminds us, *For he that will love life, and see good days, let him refrain his tongue from evil, and his lips that they speak no guile.*

This simply means *you better watch what you say!*

Have you recently found your back against the wall? Money looking funny and change is looking strange? What about your son or daughter acting out in school?

Here are some common sayings that causes us to damn our lives. These sayings and phrases are traditional talk that stems from *stinkin' thinkin'*. For far too long, we have been reaping the negative harvest of carnal talk. From talking this way, we've blocked fruitful blessings for ourselves, our children, our finances and our future.

1. I'm so broke, I can't even pay attention

2. I'm so sick, I feel like I'm about to die

3. Don't look like we'll ever get the house

4. We sneeze and say I'm coming down with something *(as if a bad cough indicates the flu)*

5. Well, it looks like I'm going to be single all my life

6. I can't get a job because of my (*criminal*) record

7. You won't ever be anything in life, just like your daddy

8. We're not going to have any money for Christmas this year *(mind you, this is being said in July)*

9. I love you to death

10. Our kids won't even be able to go to college
(mind you, said while kids are only in Middle School)

11. My husband will never change

Beloved, this is why your back has been against that brick wall and the reason why your change is looking strange! Traditional talk consists of the things we may say everyday which is why we feel they are harmless. Perhaps, maybe you don't speak this way, but you hear others speaking such venom, on a daily basis.

Humanly, we don't pay much attention to our words, because as stated earlier, we've been taught that "*sticks and stones may break my bones, but words will never hurt me!*" However, as you see through the scriptures and (*maybe*) from personal experience, words CURSE your future and ultimately causes death!

Throughout the book, we have read examples of how our words can damn us.

There was a great legend that often played the actor's role of holding his chest, *acting* as if he was having a massive attack. After years of playing that role, the actor suffered cardiac arrest and died in the 1990s.

An infamous rapper that was murdered in 1996 at the young age of 25. Many assume that the rapper spoke his own death simply because death was a recurring theme in his music. Unbelievably, the young artist gave details about how he would be taken from time to his eternal destination. One evening, the words that he frequently rapped in his lyrics came to past.

Before you picked up this book, you may have been one who believed that *words* are just *words*. Have you ever sat and thought about how the mere uttering of words have set moods, inspired us, encouraged us, comforted us, and even stirred us up! Surely if words causes such emotions, they also have the same power to negatively manifest gloomy outcomes in our lives.

We must realize that we *really* are what we say and that our kids become what we call them. Knowing this, let us change the way we speak! Though we think that words are *no big deal*, they really are! Depending on our emotional and mental state, words have the power to make or break us!

Through my *Right Talk, Right Results* Master Class, I encourage my students to counter their negative sayings with fruitful words that are filled with life! The list of common sayings given in this chapter have positive ways to actually say them!

You are probably pondering how can this be? These are *facts*! Allow me to walk you through the steps of how to turn the negative day-to-day sayings into positive ones.

When we define *facts*, we refer to them as the association with real, demonstrable existence. Facts are *actual*! [True that!] <u>BUT</u> there is a truth that is greater than our facts! As believers, we should never exhort our facts over the truth of God's Word. To the natural man, we are challenged within ourselves to believe that we are in denial when we do not acknowledge that symptoms are present. However, living *by faith* empowers us to believe without manifestation of evidence.

For example, when we sneeze, have the chills, and a runny nose, the symptoms lead us to believe that we really are coming down with the flu. Therefore, we say it. We can combat the self-diagnosis with proclaiming, "I'm sneezing, I have a runny nose and the chills, but I am healed!

Of course, we must utilize the resources to help reduce and diminish the symptoms, but we should not self- diagnosis. Especially without a nasal or throat swab. Beloved, it is unwise to give yourself a diagnosis based solely off symptoms without a medical degree. This is an example of how we've become DAMNED by our words and literally have *talked* ourselves into a professional influenza diagnosis.

So, here it is – straight; without chaser or any preservatives, it comes to this; though we can acknowledge the facts, we should never allow the facts *(big or little)* to take precedence over God's Word.

In the process of acknowledging the facts, be sure to include the word <u>BUT!</u> We understand this word being a conjunction! This my friends is very, very vital. When we incorporate BUT amidst acknowledging facts (or symptoms), we are able to rebut the negative with this 3-letter word! For example, I am hurting, and my body is rocking in pain, <u>BUT</u> I am healed! Though we recognize the symptoms, our faith (God's Word) supersedes our current state. In addition, we must execute the necessary actions that align with our new talk! Although we would love to eat whatever we want, multiples times a day, we cannot denounce hypertension and proclaim total healing, yet continue living an unhealthy lifestyle.

My hope is that by reading this book, you will apply the biblical principles and examples given to your everyday talk. By doing this, you will see a shift in everything around you and you will no longer be HUNG BY YOUR TONGUE!

HUNG BY YOUR TONGUE	SPEAKING LIFE
I'M SO BROKE, I CAN'T EVEN PAY ATTENTION	MY FINANCES AREN'T WHERE I WANT THEM TO BE, BUT I HAVE CREATED A BUDGET THAT I WILL STICK TO!
I'M SO SICK, I FEEL LIKE I'M ABOUT TO DIE	I AM NOT FEELING WELL, BUT I AM HEALED!
DON'T LOOK LIKE WE ARE GOING TO EVER GET THE HOUSE	IT'S TAKING SOME TIME TO GET THE HOUSE, BUT WE ARE ON THE RIGHT TRACK TO GETTING IT!
WELL, IT LOOKS LIKE I'M GOING TO BE SINGLE ALL MY LIFE	I'M SINGLE, BUT, I KNOW THAT MR. OR MRS. RIGHT IS AWAITING ME!
I CAN'T GET A JOB BECAUSE OF MY RECORD	I DON'T HAVE A JOB YET, BUT I KNOW THAT I WILL GET ONE SOON, DESPITE WHAT MY RECORD LOOKS LIKE!
(CHILD'S NAME), YOU WON'T EVER BE ANYTHING IN LIFE, JUST LIKE YOUR DADDY	(CHILD'S NAME), BABY, YOU ARE A KING! YOU WERE CREATED TO DO GREAT THINGS, YOU ARE GOING THROUGH A PHASE!
WE'RE NOT GOING TO HAVE ANY MONEY FOR CHRISTMAS THIS YEAR (SAID IN JULY)	MONEY IS LOOKING FUNNY, BUT OUR FINANCES WILL BE MULTIPLIED!
I LOVE YOU TO DEATH	I LOVE YOU TO LIFE!
OUR KIDS WON'T EVEN BE ABLE TO GO TO COLLEGE	OUR KIDS WILL OBTAIN A SCHOLARSHIP TO PAY FOR THEIR COLLEGE!
MY HUSBAND WILL NEVER CHANGE	BY FAITH, MY HUSBAND IS ALL THAT GOD CREATED HIM TO BE! A PROVIDER AND PROTECTOR!

Proverbs 15:28

The heart of the righteous weighs its answers, but the mouth of the wicked gushes evil

CHAPTER 7
OH SAY AND YOU'LL SEE

I can remember back in 2007 or so, God empowered me to teach a series entitled, *Oh Say and You'll See*. This series was predicated upon the principle in the first chapter of Genesis. Repeatedly, this chapter outlined the things that *God said*, followed by what God saw. For example, ***Genesis 1:3, And God said, Let there be light: and there was light.*** The very thing that God spoke, came to past.

My intention with this series was to encourage my congregation to *speak* the Word of God in faith with corresponding actions to get the results that you desire.

There are many instances in my own life that I have spoken and taken the necessary actions to manifest the outcome that I desired. For example, I wanted my own trucking company. I said it and saw it! I have also spoken this very book into existence. I knew the book's title and the content that I wanted to share. After speaking it and putting forth the actions, I finally see it. I released my faith and followed through with the actions!

Oh Say and You'll See is a promise. Whatever you say, you shall also see. My prayer is that you will learn to say and speak all things positive and the things that are filled with light and life daily. The seeds we sow through our words, are sure to manifest that same harvest.

At times, our circumstances may cause us to believe that the things we desire are so farfetched, however, as believers, we know that faith is now, according to **Hebrews 11:1**, *Now faith is the substance of things hoped for, the evidence of things not seen.*

I remember back in the 1990's when my mom was living. I called to check on her as she was planning to travel to Georgia to be with her sisters. She informed me that she was no longer going because the doctors found a lump in her breast. Although I was on the phone with her, I sensed the anxiety and felt her weariness through the tone of her voice. Immediately, my wife and I went to see my mom and I prayed for her. I encouraged my mother to exercise her faith and though she acknowledged the doctors report, as a believer of God's Word, she was to *call it*, how she wanted the results to be. **Romans 4:17** commands us, *Calleth those things which be not as though they were.* Literally, we said it, and we saw it! Upon her follow-up visit, the doctors were puzzled as to where the mass had *mysteriously* gone.

This is a vivid moment in my life where I called what was not, as though I wanted it to be, and encouraged my mother to do the same.

By faith, we can speak and live the life we desire. In **Hebrews 11:3** the scripture says, *Through faith we understand that the worlds were framed by the Word of God, so that things which are seen were not made of things which do appear.*

All in all, with the words that you speak, an outcome will be death or life. It is evident that you will be either DAMNED, or blessed if you say it. As we have learned, according to **Matthew 12:37**, *For by thy words thou shalt be justified, and by thy words thou shalt be condemned.*

Our words. Our choice. Are you going to *damn* your future, or will you speak life and blessings upon it?

Now that you have taken the time to examine your word choice, hopefully you will also commit to choosing to speak fruitful words.

Let's dive a little deeper into how words can make or break our vision. When we understand this concept, we are more deliberate in making sure that what we say reflects what we would REALLY like to see happen in our lives.

I know there are some things that you'd like to see happen in your life. Perhaps the things you want are being cancelled out by the thoughts you entertain in your mind.

Sometimes, the things we say are done in routine and without the adequate knowledge of how powerful the words we release really are.

After exploring the common phrases in the *Hung By Your Tongue* chapter, make an effort you to retrain your mind by utilizing the alternative word choices in the *'How To Speak Life'* column on page 59.

This part requires self-reflection and mirror insight into what you really want. Once you understand the power of your words, you can now use them to your advantage. Despite what you have gone thru in life, you have the power to shift your entire future outcomes by speaking what you desire. Of course, you must also be intentional and take actionable steps to manifest that which you've spoken. No matter if you've been molested, gone thru a horrible divorce, a terrible breakup, or even had to file bankruptcy, you have to realize that your *purpose is greater than your pain.*

I want you to use your words to design your life just as God designed the world with the power of His words.

Knowing what you want out of life is the first step. Once you're clear on your life's direction, you can speak in agreement with where you desire to grow and go.

Take a moment to reflect and write! Remember, no goal is too big or farfetched!

WHAT IS YOUR ULTIMATE GOAL IN LIFE?
(You can make a list of the things you desire in life)

_____

_____

_____

_____

_____

_____

_____

_____

_____

_____

NOW, LIST THE ACTIONS THAT YOU BELIEVE
ARE NECESSARY TO MAKE THOSE GOALS A
REALITY. *(For example, if you listed purchasing a home, you would
first have to have good credit. If you are working to re-build your credit,
you could list, repair credit and budget or hire a credit specialist)*

_____

_____

_____

_____

_____

_____

_____

_____

_____

Beloved, if you've found yourself struggling to answer the above, it's likely that you have *Stinkin' Thinkin'*! See how the mind and perhaps, our current state can tarnish how we envision our future and our goals?

Sometimes, your current situation can stunt your mindset from thinking and dreaming big! You were probably just about to write down big goals but couldn't fathom them based on what you're currently going through. However, as you have learned, *Stinkin' Thinkin'* causes you to be *Hung By Your Tongue*, ultimately causing you to sabotage your own self. It makes you dwell on questions like, *how can I even accomplish this?* You center your thoughts around things you don't have, who you don't know, what you lack and overall scarcity. *Stinkin' Thinkin'* robs you of the opportunity to create a bigger vision for your life.

Now, if this was the case for you while you were answering the above questions, what I want you to do is, remove any limits and any doubts. Don't contemplate on what you lack. None of that matters. The Word of God encourages us that He has already made provisions for our vision. **2 Peter 1:3** encourages us, *According as his divine* *power hath given unto us all things that pertain unto life and godliness.*

God doesn't operate in cannot because He is a God that CAN. Since we are created in His image, we are joint heirs.

In **Philippians 4:13**, we are inspired to know, *I can do all things through Christ which strengthens me.* This scripture reminds us of the power that we have been given through Christ Jesus.

Again, whether you think you CAN or CANNOT; YOU ARE RIGHT.

This is why it is so important that we are wise in your word choices, thought cycles and life directions.

Through this book, I want you to change the trajectory of your thoughts. Changing your thoughts will cause you to speak words of life and positivity. This type of lifestyle will enable you to think bigger, talk better and to expect more for your life. When you expect more for your life, you execute and take action to fulfil the things that you desire!

Perhaps, you may need a little direction figuring out what your ultimate goals in life are. I believe that by stating your short-term goals, it will help you identify your ultimate goal(s). Ultimate or long-term goals are the things that take a long time to achieve. Short-term goals, however, are the things you'd want to do in the near future. The near future can mean today, within a week, a month, or even this year. A short-term goal is something you'd like to accomplish soon.

We can even start with identifying what would make your life better!

WHAT DOES A BETTER LIFE FOR YOU LOOK LIKE? *(for example, perhaps you did not complete high school, you could list complete my GED)*

_____

_____

_____

_____

_____

_____

_____

_____

_____

SHORT-TERM GOALS *(list the things you would like to accomplish in the coming weeks, within a month or within a year)*

_____

_____

_____

_____

_____

_____

_____

_____

_____

ULTIMATE / LONG-TERM GOALS *(list the things you would like to accomplish in life)*

_____

_____

_____

_____

_____

_____

_____

_____

_____

Did you really take time to write your goals? This exercise is to help you!

It's challenging to achieve what you cannot see. In **Habakkuk 2:2** it urges us, *Write the vision, and make it plain.*

If you failed to complete it, go back! Write down your goals so that when you review them, you will be fueled to complete them!

Now that you have taken time to get clear and identify what you want for your life, I want you to create personal declarations that affirm what you want. This helps you to practice talking right.

You can start by making a list of five daily affirmations. Affirmations are desired confessions of the things we want to manifest in our lives.

Remember, what you desire, after speaking it, you must take actionable steps to make it happen! Your affirmations should align with your goals!

The goal of this exercise is to make *speaking life* a habit. *Oh Say and You'll See*! In life, whatsoever you speak *(and do)*, those fruit will manifest.

Examples of my daily affirmations are:

> *I'm out of debt, and all my needs are met!*
> *I am the above and not the beneath!*
> *I am the lender and not the borrower!*
> *I have plenty to give to many!*
> *I am the well and not the sick!*

LIST YOUR AFFIRMATIONS HERE:

1. _____

_____

2. _____

_____

3. _____

_____

4. _____

_____

5. _____

_____

Just as simply *listing* your short-term goals is only one component of making the goals a reality, *speaking* daily affirmations is only one component in fulfilling that which is spoken.

You may want to establish a business. While writing it down and speaking it into existence is necessary, again, ACTION is required!

I want you to repeat and affirm for 21 days what you desire to manifest! After 21 days, examine your progress. This is simply seeing what you have said!

For example, if one of your affirmation was *"I am a business owner,"* because you desire to start a business, your progression would consist of you purchasing a your Incorporation (Inc.) or Limited Liability Corporation (LLC) thru the state.

Beloved, remember, speaking it is only one component. It would be great if all we had to do to obtain what we desire was to *"name it, aim it and claim it,"* however, we must execute corresponding actions!

Habakkuk 2:2

Write the vision, and make it plain.

CHAPTER 8
SEED TIME — HARVEST TIME

S eed-time, harvest-time is an inevitable aspect of life. In **Genesis 8:22**, *While the earth remaineth, seedtime and harvest, and cold and heat, and summer and winter, and day and night shall not cease.*

God's promise is that the seasons will always be with us. Because God *said* it, this is a principle that we can count on. Though this scripture pertains to nature's four seasons and their respective climates, the concept also translates to words that are spoken in our lives.

How? Simply because our words are just like seeds. The things we say *(seeds)* are then cultivated by beliefs and actions.

Have you ever heard family members call their children bad? "(*Child's Name) is so bad, he's just a little Tasmanian devil.*" Those words are then cultivated by repeated accounts of the parent calling their child *bad* and before we know it, in their teenage years, the child has become a convicted felon. This is a prime example of seed-time, harvest-time. The seeds that were sown in this example were filled with negativity, followed by a teenaged, convicted felon being the harvest.

Luke 8:11 says, *"Now the parable is this: The seed is the word of God."* This principle confirms that what we say, as believers, must always relate to God's Word. This way, we can be assured that the harvest, will always be fruitful. We understand that this principle is confirmed by a time to sow; seed-time, and a time to reap; harvest-time.

Recognizing the true power in this, we can decide to sow productive seeds to reap a productive harvest. I am reminded that every seed shall produce its own kind. Outlined in **Galatians 6:7**, *Be not deceived; God is not mocked: for whatsoever a man soweth, that shall he also reap,* vividly affirms the principle of seed-time, harvest-time.

Have you ever seen orange seeds or apple seeds? Orange seeds are white, and apple seeds are dark brown or   black.

When we plant orange seeds, we cannot expect apples to grow from that tree, just as when we plant apple seeds, we should not expect oranges to grow. In relation to our words, we cannot speak words of failure and expect success.

You cannot get around the unwavering life principle of seed-time, harvest-time. Therefore, it requires us to develop good farming skills. During my research, I learned that one of the good qualities of a farmer is understanding the cultivation and irrigation aspect of it.

During the initial phase of planting, a farmer cultivates the seed. Cultivation is the process in determining the best outcome for the seeds. This consists of the work that goes into making the seeds better. In this period, farmers choose the grounds in which they will plant seeds and discover the soil type to determine how the planted seeds should be irrigated.

To gain a substantial return, it is important for us to cultivate and irrigate. This within itself, gives us the expectation that we will produce the best harvest. In **Proverbs 4:23**, the Word encourages us, *"Keep thy heart with all diligence; for out of it are the issues of life."*

Think of yourself as a farmer; sowing seeds through what you speak. As farmers, it is also important for us to monitor the grounds that we have sowed upon, even after the seeds have been planted. This scripture motivates us to guard our hearts and helps us to put in perspective the importance of choosing words that are filled with life.

In the irrigation phase, farmers determine the cycle and systems of how seeds will be watered. This is a pertinent phase because irrigation will influence the entire growth process. With successful irrigation, as farmers, we anticipate a plentiful harvest.

Because we know that irrigation is a form of watering, in terms of our words, we must speak the words that we have sowed, faithfully. In **Jeremiah 23:28,** *"And he that hath my word, let him speak my word faithfully."* This is, of course, speaking *life* and *light*!

Remember, seed-time, harvest-time is an inevitable principle. Be very careful how you sow your seeds! You are promised to reap a harvest and you do not want to harvest a crop that you did not intend to plant!

We are the farmers of our lives and in the lives of our children. If we want success for our children, we must sow seeds of excellence and greatness. Seed-time, harvest-time is simple; that which you sow, you shall also reap!

Galatians
6:7

Be not deceived; God is not mocked: for whatsoever a man soweth, that shall he also reap

CHAPTER 9
A TIME TO SPEAK

S aying the right words is such a powerful phenomenon. The right words can design a life that we love. While speaking *right* can propel us into a desired destiny, one thing we have to be mindful of is the timing of our word selection.

The truth is, even the right words at the wrong time can be problematic. So now that you understand the power of words, and you've made a conscious decision to change the way you speak, let's explore the concept of timing and gaining the wisdom to not only say the right things, but to know when to say the right things at the right time.

I would like to share a story with you about to illustrate the essence of a time to speak.

Mary was a gentle and kind woman, she was the first person in the community to welcome new neighbors with a fresh home cooked apple pie, the first to volunteer at PTA meetings and when families suffered any type of hardship, she was the first to offer her help. Mary was known to be a woman of wise and comforting words, in fact, her reputation within the community was that Mary was a good woman.

One afternoon, there was a U-Haul truck pulling into the corner lot on Mary's street. In true Mary fashion, she whipped up a fresh batch of homemade oatmeal and chocolate chip cookies. Her famous recipe was known for winning over new friends. Once Mary had pulled the cookies out of the oven she let them cool. After they cooled, she placed them in a beautiful basket with a handwritten, *Welcome to the Neighborhood* note.

As she walked over to greet the new neighbors, she was greeted by a young man and a young woman. They were walking outside to head to the U-Haul and unload more items.

Mary offered the family the warm cookies, introduced herself and started a casual and friendly conversation with the young couple. Mary then asked where the family had moved from since it was the middle of the year, it seemed that they had moved rather abruptly. The young man answered that life had forced them into a new direction and that they were in a re-building phase, piecing life back together. Mary then noticed a baby crib and some baby furniture on the back of the U-Haul truck. With a bit of excitement because she assumed that they were welcoming a new baby she exclaimed, *"Whatever you're going through, I'm sure your new bundle of joy will make your transition a bit smoother."*

Immediately, the young woman burst into tears and ran inside the home. The young man apologized for his wife and explained to Mary that they had suffered the loss of their baby. He shared that his wife was having an extremely hard time dealing with the sudden death of their baby and they decided that moving into a new home would help them with the healing process. In their transition, however, they had not been able to let go of the baby's furniture.

Mary felt horrible. As a woman of love and kindness, obviously, it was not her intent to hurt the grieving mother in any way. In fact, she thought that she was using words of comfort when she made the statement.

If Mary had made that statement during a different time or setting, it may not have had the same effect on the grief-stricken mother as it did. This is a great example of how kind words can be painful if used at the wrong time.

We never know what people are going through or what secret battles they are fighting. It is important to never make assumptions.

Instead of Mary making the assumption that the young couple had a new baby that would bring them joy in their dark hour, she could have simply led with a question after seeing the baby furniture, like, *"Do you guys have any children?"* The couple may have then informed her of their recent tragedy. Perhaps it could have been less painful for the mother to answer that question, than to have a stranger tell her that the pain she was experiencing would be eased by the joy of their baby, who in fact had passed away.

So, what do you say to someone who is going through a tough situation?

Often, finding the right words to say in a tough situation can be challenging. Sometimes, the best thing to say is nothing at all. **Ecclesiastes 3:7** informs us, *there a time to keep silence, and a time to speak.*

In tough situations, we should focus on what *not* to say.

When someone is facing a setback, hardship, tragedy or disappointment, it is wise to be careful not to be dismissive of their pain. Usually when someone is hurting, good words that we can say are things like, *"I am so sorry that you're hurting."* Or perhaps, we can say, *"I can't imagine what you're going through."*

We have to learn to listen without interrupting so that we can hear them out. When we do this, it allows you to get a deeper understanding so that when you do speak, you refrain from assuming and you speak with compassion and knowledge. This better prepares us to choose words that will make an impact and words that will foster hope, healing and comfort.

Our words should reflect what we believe and what we know to be true according to God's Word.

Ecclesiastes 3:7

There a time to keep silence,

and a time to speak.

CHAPTER 10
CONCLUSION

As you navigate through life and experience all that it entails, you will have those great moments when you feel incredibly blessed. There are other times when you will experience seasons when life brings you to your knees in search of God's voice or His healing touch.

No matter where life brings you or what season you may find yourself in right now, the truth of the matter is this: *God's Word gives us the tools that we need to overcome and be victorious in life.*

In fact, this is His plan for us.

The Bible is the best personal development tool that you will find on earth. Not only is it filled with wisdom, insight, and relatable stories, it even has some drama here and there. As the best resource, it equips us with ways to be resilient and teaches us how to love our enemies.

My prayer for you is that by now, you have grasped a full understanding of the power of your words and felt a conviction that has caused you to want to change how you talk. Being that you are at the end of this book, make it your priority to be more intentional with the way that you use your words. I pray that your day is filled with the affirmations that you've written, as well as actionable steps that will make what you've affirmed, a reality.

As you journey towards your best life, speak power, love, peace, prosperity, healing and righteousness over yourself, your children, your family, your neighbors, your community and your country. One thing that is certain is that there is no shortage of need. Plant seeds of faith in every hard trial and encourage your neighbors to do the same.

The words that leave your mouth take root somewhere and if those words are watered and cultivated, just like any seed, it will grow and manifest. So, make sure you choose words that represent what you want to see happen for you and in your life. Don't allow words of affliction, sickness, misery, poverty, anger, unforgiveness, hate and brokenness escape your tongue.

Even if you don't remember three scriptures references that have been given in #IBDIISI, one thing that I pray you've learned and will remember is that you'll be DAMNED if you say it!

Beloved, you have to be willing to unlearn the untruths that you've been taught. As kids, we were taught that *"sticks and stones may break my bones but words will never hurt me."* However, through the insight with Biblical reference in this book, you have learned that this saying is far from the truth.

In closing, words are the one of the most powerful sources available to humanity. We can choose to use this power constructively; choosing to use words filled with encouragement or, destructively; using words filled with desolation. I want you to recognize this power and truly understand that words have power.

Words are not just air flowing through our larynx to make a sound. When we speak, your words are either weapons of mass destruction or the tree of life.

Remember if you think you *can*, you *can* and if you think you *can't*, you *can't*.

I'll Be Damned If I Say It.

SCRIPTURES TO HELP YOU IN YOUR JOURNEY
TO BE MORE INTENTIONAL IN SPEAKING LIFE,
NO MATTER THE SITUATION

Job 6:24
Teach me, and I will be quiet;
show me where I have been wrong.

Psalms 19:14
May these words of my mouth and this
meditation of my heart be pleasing in your sight,
Lord, my Rock and my Redeemer.

Psalms 141:3
Set a guard over my mouth, Lord;
keep watch over the door of my lips.

Proverbs 15:1
A gentle answer turns away wrath,
but a harsh word stirs up anger.

Proverbs 15:4
The soothing tongue is a tree of life,
but a perverse tongue crushes the spirit.

Proverbs 18:21
The tongue has the power of life and death,
and those who love it will eat its fruit.

Matthew 12:36-37
But I tell you that everyone will have to give account
on the day of judgment for every empty word they have
spoken. For by your words you will be acquitted, and
by your words you will be condemned.

James 3:1-11
Not many of you should become teachers, my fellow
believers, because you know that we who teach will be
judged more strictly. We all stumble in many ways.
Anyone who is never at fault in what they say is
perfect, able to keep their whole body in check.

When we put bits into the mouths of horses to make
them obey us, we can turn the whole animal. Or take
ships as an example. Although they are so large and are
driven by strong winds, they are steered by a very small
rudder wherever the pilot wants to go. Likewise, the
tongue is a small part of the body, but it makes great
boasts. Consider what a great forest is set on fire by a
small spark. The tongue also is a fire, a world of evil
among the parts of the body. It corrupts the whole body,
sets the whole course of one's life on fire, and is itself
set on fire by hell.

All kinds of animals, birds, reptiles and sea creatures
are being tamed and have been tamed by mankind, but
no human being can tame the tongue. It is a restless
evil, full of deadly poison. With the tongue we praise
our Lord and Father, and with it we curse human

beings, who have been made in God's likeness. Out of the same mouth come praise and cursing. My brothers and sisters, this should not be. Can both fresh water and salt water flow from the same spring?

ABOUT THE AUTHOR

Bishop Al Cook is a prolific speaker, teacher, husband, father, grandfather, mentor and believer of God's Word. As pastor, he has passion to teach God's people. With his unique blend of humor, simplicity, transparency, and everyday living examples, Bishop Cook continues to win souls for Christ. He believes that his God-given purpose in life is to minister the gospel of God's love and faithfulness. As a steward of the Word of God, he helps build, strengthen, and restore the character of others through his *Right Talk, Right Results* Master Class, *Marriage Made Right 411* Couples Ministry and mentorship.

CONNECT WITH BISHOP AL

www.AlCookSpeaks.com

EMAIL:

INFO@ALCOOKSPEAKS.COM

INSTAGRAM: @ALCOOKSPEAKS

FACEBOOK: AL COOK

TWITTER: @ALCOOKSPEAKS

YOUTUBE: AL COOK SPEAKS

If you're in Florida, come fellowship with us!

Sundays 11:00am

Mission Possible Life Church, Inc.

1140 West Main Street, Lakeland FL 33815

Live Limitless Authors Academy

Email: limitless@sierrarainge.com

www.sierrarainge.com

Made in the USA
Columbia, SC
05 September 2019